POINT OF IMPACT

Revised and Updated

Heinemann Library
Chicago, Illinois

Pearl Harbor

The US Enters World War II

Customer Service 888-454-2279
Visit our website at www.heinemannraintree.com

Designed by Tokay Interactive Ltd. (www.tokay.co.uk)
Printed in China by WKT Ltd

10 09 08 07 06
10 9 8 7 6 5 4 3 2 1

New edition ISBNs:1-40349-142-9 (hardcover)
                    1-40349-151-8 (paperback)

The Library of Congress has cataloged the first edition as follows:
Tames, Richard
    Pearl Harbor : the U.S. enters World War II / Richard Tames.
        p.cm. — (Point of Impact)
    Includes bibliographical references and index.
    Summary: Traces the rise of Japan as a military power and the emergence of the United States as a world superpower that found itself drawn into World War II after the attack on Pearl Harbor.
    ISBN 1-57572-416-2 (library binding)
    1. Pearl Harbor (Hawaii), Attack on, 1941—Juvenile literature. [1. Pearl Harbor (Hawaii), Attack on, 1941. 2. World War, 1939-1945—Causes. 3. Japan—Foreign relations—United States. 4. United States—Foreign relations—Japan.] I. Title. II. Series.

D767.92 T36 2001
940.54'26—dc21
                                                    00-024356

Acknowledgments
The publishers would like to thank the following for permission to reproduce photographs:
Corbis: pp. **9**, **14**, **17**, **20**, (Bettman) pp. **4**, **13**, **19**, **21**, **23**, (George Hall) p. **28**, (Minnesota History) p. **16**, (Museum of Flight), p. **15**, (The Marineris Museum), p. **11**; Hulton Getty: pp. **5**, **18**, **24**; Tames, Richard: pp. **6**, **7**, **10**, **25**, **27**; Tony Stone Images: p. **26**.

Cover photograph reproduced with permission of Empics / AP Photo.

The publishers would like to thank Stewart Ross for his help in the preparation of this book.

Every effort has been made to contact copyright holders of any material reproduced in this book. Any omissions will be rectified in subsequent printings if notice is given to the publisher.

The paper used to print this book comes from sustainable resources.

Contents

Some words are shown in bold, **like this**. You can find out what they mean by looking in the Glossary.

Tora! Tora! Tora!

Total surprise

At dawn on Sunday, December 7, 1941, Japanese aircraft launched a surprise attack on Pearl Harbor, the U.S. naval base in Hawaii. Sweeping in from carriers out at sea, they wrecked 21 ships, over 300 planes, and caused 3,500 **casualties**. The Japanese lost just 29 planes, 5 small submarines, and 64 men. The strike had come without warning, with a declaration of war being made only after it had started. To the United States, it was not simply **aggression**—it was **treachery**.

Retreat from victory

The Japanese failed to hit three U.S. aircraft carriers out at sea. Not knowing the position of these ships, the Japanese feared a counterattack. Rather than risk a third attack against Pearl Harbor's oil stores and repair facilities, the Japanese sailed home.

The country unites

Until Pearl Harbor was attacked, many Americans wanted to stay out of the wars raging in Europe and Asia. Pearl Harbor enraged U.S. opinion.

Of the 1,400 crew of the USS *Arizona*, 1,102 were killed. The wreck is now an official war grave. Most of the other ships that were sunk or damaged were repaired to fight again.

Sleeping giant

While his fellow soldiers celebrated, Admiral Yamamoto Isoroku, planner of the attack, warned grimly, "I fear we have only awakened a sleeping giant and his reaction will be terrible." Yamamoto, a former naval **attaché** in Washington, D.C., had opposed war with the United States.

This newspaper appeared on the Hawaiian island of Oahu within 90 minutes of Japan's attack on Pearl Harbor. The final death toll was much higher than stated in the headlines.

Eyewitness

John Garcia, who was sixteen at the time, was a civilian engineer. He remembers the attack and the events that followed:

"I spent the day swimming . . . I brought out I don't know how many bodies . . . The following morning I went with my tools to the *West Virginia*. It had turned turtle, totally upside down . . .

"About 300 men we cut out of there were still alive by the eighteenth day. It took two weeks to get all the fires out. . . . they told me a shell had hit the house of my girl . . . they said it was a Japanese bomb. Later we learned it was an American shell. She was killed . . . getting ready for church."

President Franklin D. Roosevelt declared to Congress:

"Yesterday, December 7, 1941—a date that will live in **infamy**—the United States of America was suddenly and deliberately attacked by . . . the **Empire** of Japan . . . our people, our territory, and our interests are in grave danger . . . With confidence in our armed forces . . . we will gain the inevitable triumph. So help us God."

Opening Up Japan

Japan meets the West: Part 1

Japan had no contact with Western countries until Portuguese ships arrived there in 1543. A century of trade followed, which brought in new technology, such as clocks and guns. From 1639 Japan closed off contact with the outside world, gaining security from intruders but falling behind in technology.

Japan meets the West: Part 2

War against Mexico (1846–48) brought California under U.S. control. From there, Americans wanted to trade with China. In 1853 the U.S. Navy forced Japan—at gunpoint—to open up its seaports for U.S. ships to buy food and water, for repair, and for trade. Over the next half century, Japan imported Western technology and institutions in order to transform itself into a modern industrial and military power.

In 1850 Yokohama was a tiny fishing village of wooden houses. By 1875 it had Western-style stone buildings and Japan's first railroad.

Enrich the country! Strengthen the army!

Unlike the government of its great neighbor, China, which tried to ignore Western powers, Japan's leaders saw the West as both a threat and an opportunity. Japan adopted a Western-style calendar, coinage, postal system, and weights and measures. German instructors trained the new army. The British built the first railroad in Japan, trained the navy, and supplied its ships. U.S. advisors reformed education and agriculture. By the 1890s, Japan had its own steel mills and shipyards and no longer needed foreign experts. To avoid becoming a **colony** of one of the expanding Western empires, Japan became powerful enough to create an empire of its own.

The battleship *Mikasa* was the flagship of Admiral Togo during the battle of Tsushima (below). Built in England, the vessel had been launched in 1902.

Japan emerges

Victory over China in 1894–95 brought Japan rice-rich Taiwan as her first colony. In 1902 Great Britain became Japan's **ally**. This enabled Japan to defeat Russia and gain control of Korea in 1904–05 because Britain kept France, Russia's ally, out of the war. Japanese sea-power was decisive in both these victories. Successful wars made the armed forces popular and powerful in Japan.

The Russo–Japanese War, 1904–05

The Russo–Japanese War for Korea began with the Japanese navy trapping the Russian Pacific fleet in its base at Port Arthur in China. On land the two sides fought to a standstill. Meanwhile Russia's Baltic fleet sailed more than halfway around the world to join in. When it reached the Straits of Tsushima in May 1905, Admiral Togo Heihachiro's Japanese fleet conquered the Russian fleet in hours. After that, Russia agreed to peace.

Expanding the United States

From east to west

Colonial America was settled from Europe by sea and prospered from seaborne trade. Arguments over taxes on that trade led to the war for American independence that began in 1775. That war led to the United States forming its first navy. Americans then spread westward, controlling California by 1849. Now possessing both western and eastern seaboards, they looked to trade with Pacific Asia as well as with Europe.

An admiral's advice

In 1890 U.S. Admiral A. T. Mahan wrote a book called *The Influence of Sea-Power on History*. In it he argued that Britain owed its worldwide empire to its navy. The U.S. Navy, important in the U.S. Civil War (1861–65), had been neglected. Mahan recommended that the United States restore its navy, acquire overseas bases, and build a canal through Central America for ships to pass from the Atlantic to the Pacific without going around South America. This would cut the journey from the Caribbean to California by three-quarters, saving 7,000 miles (11,250 kilometers) and six weeks.

The inset location map shows where maps 1 and 2 are. The yellow shows U.S. expansion, 1867–1914. Areas too small to show clearly are underlined in yellow. Map 1 shows Guam, Wake, Midway, the Hawaiian islands, and Samoa. Map 2 shows the Panama Canal, Puerto Rico, and Guantanamo (Cuba).

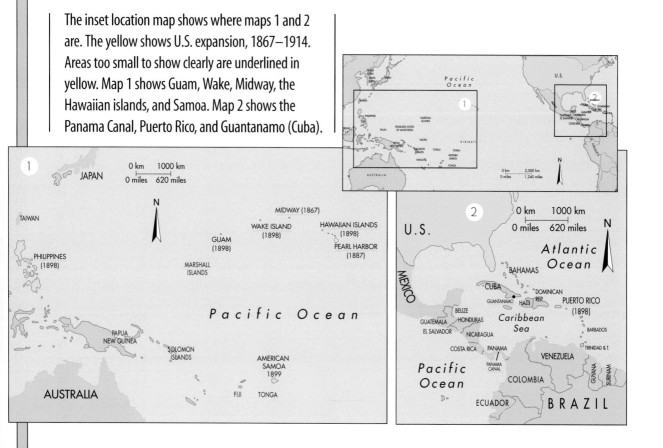

A new power at sea

The United States listened to Mahan. By 1900 the U.S. Navy had grown from twelfth to third largest in the world. U.S. naval power was shown in the Spanish–American War of 1898. At Manila Bay, Commodore George Dewey's six modern ships sank ten outdated Spanish ships without losing a single man. Off Cuba, another U.S. fleet lost just one sailor in destroying a second Spanish fleet. This war gave the United States control of the Philippines, Puerto Rico, and the Pacific island of Guam and the right to build a naval base in Cuba. In 1898 the U.S. also took over Hawaii. In 1908 it began building a naval base at Pearl Harbor. Between 1907 and 1909, the U.S. Navy's "Great White Fleet" of sixteen battleships sailed about 46,000 miles (73,600 kilometers) around the world in a show of strength.

The Panama Canal

Building a canal through Panama started in 1882. It only succeeded after an environmental cleanup of swamps and undergrowth in 1904–06 wiped out mosquitoes carrying **yellow fever** and rats carrying **plague**. The U.S. Corps of Army Engineers completed the 51-mile- (82-kilometer-) long canal between 1908 and 1914 for $380,000,000. Thanks to the canal, the U.S. Navy could switch its strength quickly to either the Pacific or Atlantic Ocean. The canal is now too small for most modern aircraft carriers.

Pacific Rivals

World War 1...

As Britain's ally against Germany in World War I (1914–18), Japan used its navy to capture the German-controlled Shandong area of China and German colonies in the Pacific (the Mariana, Caroline, and Marshall Islands). Japan kept the islands after the war ended in 1918. German U-boat sinkings of **neutral** U.S. ships helped bring the United States into the war in 1917 as one of Britain's allies.

...and after

At the 1919 Paris Peace Conference, U.S. President Woodrow Wilson launched the League of Nations, with the aim of settling disputes between countries peacefully. Unfortunately, Wilson, a dying man, could not get the United States itself to join, and this weakened the League. The League also refused to adopt a declaration of racial equality suggested by Japan. The Japanese felt that, despite all their efforts to modernize their country, they were still not accepted as equals by Westerners.

Britain's Prince of Wales poses with Japanese naval officers in 1921. The twenty-year-old Anglo–Japanese alliance ended that year. The United States could now fight Japan without coming into conflict with Britain.

The USS *Saratoga* was converted from a battle-cruiser that had been scrapped in accordance with the 1922 Washington Naval Agreement.

The United States and Japan

At the Washington Naval Conference, organized by the United States in 1921–22, Japan was persuaded to agree that, for every five battleships the United States and Britain had, it would have only three. The United States and Britain agreed not to strengthen bases west of Pearl Harbor, giving Japan superiority in its home waters. The Anglo–Japanese **alliance** was dissolved after twenty years. This ended U.S. fears that, in a war with Japan, the United States might risk fighting Britain, too.

In 1924 Congress passed a law against Japanese **immigration** to the United States. The Japanese took this as a further insult by the West.

The aircraft carrier

Carriers were pioneered during World War I. The first were ordinary warships converted to carry seaplanes. Carriers with flight decks were in service by 1917. Japan's first specially built carrier, the *Hosho*, was launched in 1922. Larger ships soon followed. The USS *Lexington* and *Saratoga* and the Japanese *Akagi* and *Kaga*, all conversions, were completed in 1927–28. In the 1930s, the United States, Japan, and Britain were the only nations to begin building large specially built carriers. The USS *Yorktown* carried 80 planes, the Japanese *Shokaku* 84, and the HMS *Illustrious* only 55—but the British design was much better armored and stronger.

The Americans and Japanese thought carrier-borne planes in large numbers could cripple an enemy fleet at distances far beyond those of a battleship's guns. World War II was to prove them right and make the battleship **obsolete**. Pearl Harbor was one of the battles to show this.

A World Without Work

Making jobs

The collapse of world trade between 1929 and 1931 caused mass unemployment in all the industrial nations. Japan was still recovering from a terrible earthquake that had wrecked Tokyo in 1923, killing over 100,000 people. In the United States, conditions were made worse by droughts, which turned rich farmlands into "dust bowls." From 1933 onward, President Roosevelt's "New Deal" program tried to put Americans back to work by funding conservation and building projects. In Germany, Adolf Hitler's **Nazi** government created jobs by building roads and rearming for a future war.

Making trouble

Japan had few minerals, no oil or rubber and, being very mountainous, had too many farmers for too little land. **Extremists**, especially in the army, favored expanding the overseas empire by war. This would give Japan access to the raw materials it lacked, markets for its manufacturers, and land on which to settle its growing population. Civilian politicians who said they wanted cooperation with the West rather than war put their lives at risk. When Japan agreed to the London Naval **Treaty** (1930), putting new limits on naval building, Prime Minister Hamaguchi was **assassinated** at the Tokyo Railroad Station.

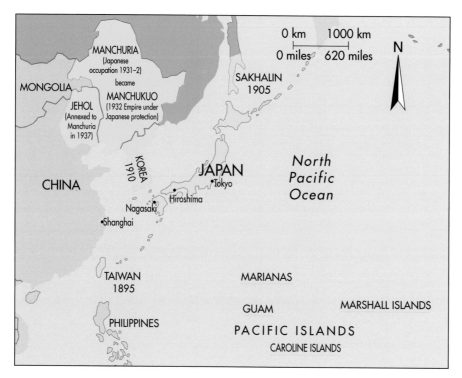

Yellow areas show Japanese expansion in the period 1894–1937. Islands that are too small to be seen are underlined in yellow.

Manchuria becomes Manchukuo

In 1931, without asking permission from the civilian government in Tokyo, Japanese generals ordered troops into the resource-rich Chinese province of Manchuria. In 1932 they set up a **puppet government**, pretending the area was the independent state of Manchukuo. When the League of Nations condemned the invasion as aggression, Japan left the League in 1933. In 1934 Puyi, China's last emperor and a Manchu, was made emperor of Manchukuo. Real power, however, remained in Japanese hands. In 1937 Japanese troops from Manchukuo began a full-scale invasion of the rest of China.

Puyi, the top-hatted puppet ruler of Manchukuo, is surrounded by Japanese generals and officials.

The February 26, 1936, incident

In 1936 junior army officers used 1,400 troops to seize the Japanese **parliament** and prime minister's home. They assassinated two ministers and a general and demanded a new government. The rebellion was crushed in days and nineteen leaders were shot. However, the army used the uprising to increase its power over government, arguing that this was the only way discontent among junior officers could be controlled. In 1938 a National **Mobilization** Bill geared business up for all-out war production, giving the government strict control over companies, **trade unions**, prices, and the media.

Edging Toward World War

War in China

By December 1937, Japanese troops had taken Beijing, Shanghai, and Nanjing, where at least 150,000 civilians were massacred. Western eyewitnesses were horrified but helpless. When Japanese planes sank the U.S. gunboat *Panay*, which was carrying Chinese **refugees** near Nanjing, Japan apologized and paid $2,000,000 in compensation. The United States accepted this.

A Chinese baby screams amid the wreckage of a Shanghai railroad station bombed by the Japanese.

Although the United States had accepted Japanese apologies, it wanted Japan to stop the aggression against China. However, U.S. public opinion still favored staying out of foreign wars and concentrating on getting people back to work after the **Great Depression**. Besides, Japan had an army of two million, while the United States' was under 200,000. Although Japanese naval tonnage was only 70 percent of the United States', its carrier tonnage was 94 percent of the United States'.

The United States could hardly threaten war if it was not prepared to rearm. Japan was divided over the risks of action. A panel of bankers and military advisors estimated the U.S. economy to be ten times as productive as Japan's. On the other hand, Japanese generals saw the United States as a country of movie stars, gangsters, and jazz, not soldiers. They believed it would protest over China, but do nothing.

A U.S. bomber factory: the Japanese greatly underestimated the speed and size of output achieved by U.S. mass-production methods.

Alternative strategies

By 1938 the Japanese army thought its main aim should be to finish conquering China and confront the strong **Soviet** forces on the Manchukuo border. Japan's navy favored driving into Southeast Asia to get control of supplies important for domestic industry and overseas warfare: oil, rubber, and minerals such as iron ore. This policy risked war with the British, French, Dutch, and Americans, who all had colonies or interests there.

Defeat and diplomacy

In 1938, and again in 1939, Japanese troops clashed with Soviet forces on the Manchukuo border, leading to large-scale fighting. Soviet armored units and aircraft beat the Japanese repeatedly, killing over 17,000. The Japanese army realized it was not unbeatable and decided to fight on one front at a time. Therefore, in September 1939 the Japanese asked for a ceasefire. The outbreak of war in Europe that month led the **USSR** to agree. In April 1941, the two countries agreed to remain neutral if the other went to war, thus protecting both countries from having to fight on two major fronts.

15

Hard Choices for the United States

Hoping for peace...

When Germany invaded Poland in September 1939, many Americans thought that the United States should stay out of the European war. Opinion in the United States was strongly anti-German, just as it was anti-Japanese over Asia. The Americans hoped Britain and France would be able to resist German aggression and that the the United States would reach a peaceful agreement with Japan over China.

...preparing for war

Germany crushed Poland in weeks, and in the spring of 1940 it turned west to conquer the Netherlands, Belgium, and Luxembourg. France **surrendered** in June 1940. Britain **evacuated** its troops, abandoning their equipment. U.S. generals predicted an early invasion of Britain.

Americans registered in the thousands for military service. These men are enlisting in the army. U.S. pilots, trained in three months, were known as 90-day wonders.

Japan seized the chance to take over France's colonies in Southeast Asia. As the situation worsened in both Asia and Europe, U.S. defense efforts expanded rapidly. In September 1940—for the first time in its history—the United States ordered men to register for possible military service. By December 1941, U.S. Army and Air Force manpower had risen to 1.6 million and the number of navy vessels from 1,100 to 1,900.

U.S. support

President Roosevelt believed that, despite defeats, both Britain and China would continue resistance and that U.S. security would be best served by supporting them without actually going to war.

Roosevelt pledged that the United States would be the "**arsenal** of **democracy**," supplying the weapons Britain and its allies needed to defeat the dictatorships of Hitler (in Germany) and Benito Mussolini (in Italy). This meant sending supplies to Britain and having the U.S. Navy escort the ships carrying them, even at the risk of fighting German U-boats. In China it meant supporting anti-Japanese resistance with supplies and volunteer pilots. Meanwhile, the United States banned the export of oil and scrap metal to Japan.

The Flying Tigers

The Flying Tigers were formed in April 1941 by Claire L. Chennault, a retired U.S. Army Air Corps officer and training expert. He recruited 100 pilots and 200 ground crew to help China against invading Japanese forces. They trained at a British base in Burma and defended the Chinese city of Kunming and the "Burma Road" supply route that carried supplies to Chinese troops. The Flying Tigers destroyed 286 Japanese aircraft but lost only 50 U.S. aircraft and nine pilots.

The Flying Tigers' official name was the American Volunteer Group, but the origin of their nickname is obvious in this picture.

The Great Gamble

Planning for a knockout

Faced with the United States' rapid arms buildup, Japanese leaders decided the United States meant war after all. They thought Japan's best chance of victory lay in destroying the U.S. Pacific fleet at Pearl Harbor. They believed the United States would then be unable to act to prevent the conquest of Asia for at least eighteen months. By then, Japan's new empire would be secure behind the world's biggest ocean.

Since war was unavoidable, Japanese planners wanted to start before the United States got even stronger. While Japan negotiated in Washington, Admiral Yamamoto planned his surprise attack on Pearl Harbor.

Pearl Harbor: Mistaking the dangers

U.S. forces realized an enemy first strike was possible, but it expected it would be in the Philippines, only 200 miles (320 kilometers) from Japanese-controlled Taiwan. In the remote Pacific island of Hawaii, where 150,000 local people—37 percent of the population—were of Japanese descent, the main fear was of **sabotage**.

An overhead view shows how Pearl Harbor's "Battleship Row" made an ideal target.

Looking the wrong way

Planes were therefore lined up close together to make it easier to guard them. This also made them an easier target for enemy planes. Any attack on Hawaii was expected from the Japanese-controlled Marshall Islands, 2,000 miles (3,200 kilometers) to the southwest. No long-range air **reconnaissance** was ordered, and on the morning of Sunday, December 7, 1941, most anti-aircraft guns were unmanned and without ready supplies of ammunition.

Swiftly, silently...

Yamamoto's plan depended on sailing six carriers and their support ships from Japan across 3,400 miles (5,500 kilometers) of the Pacific without being spotted. Keeping radio silence—and shielded by bad weather—the Japanese **task force** managed to sail within 280 miles (450 kilometers) of Pearl Harbor undetected and then launch its attack from the north.

A furious President Roosevelt asks Congress to declare war on Japan. The United States did so on December 8, 1941.

A diplomatic disaster

Japanese **negotiations** continued in Washington to the very end. On Saturday, December 6, there was a staff send-off party at the Japanese embassy. As a result of heavy drinking, only two senior workers were on duty the next morning when the coded message came from Tokyo carrying a formal declaration of war. Without junior workers, who were much faster at decoding and typing, the two officials failed to hand the declaration over to U.S. officials until half an hour *after* the attack on Pearl Harbor had started, instead of 30 minutes *before*, as intended. Americans were outraged.

Patriotism and Production

Relocation

In 1941 there were 120,000 people of Japanese descent (*Nisei*), two-thirds of them U.S. citizens, living on the west coast of the United States. This was where a Japanese invasion was thought most likely. Without much evidence to back it up, Japanese-Americans were suspected of disloyalty to their adopted country. So, 112,000 *Nisei* were forced to leave their homes and businesses and live in ten camps in inland states such as Arizona, Colorado, Wyoming, and Arkansas.

Despite this treatment, over 1,000 imprisoned *Nisei* volunteered to serve in the U.S. armed forces. No Japanese-Americans were proved to have taken part in spying or sabotage. In 1944 the U.S. Supreme Court ruled that relocation was **unconstitutional** and the camps were closed. Between 1948 and 1965, Japanese-Americans were paid $38,000,000 to cover their losses—less than one-tenth of what was lost. Fewer than 10,000 Americans of German or Italian descent were relocated in this manner.

Proving a point

To prove their loyalty to the United States, thousands of Japanese-Americans volunteered. A Japanese-American unit, the 100th Battalion, composed largely of Japanese-Americans born in Hawaii, won so many medals for being wounded in action that it became known as the Purple Heart Battalion. It later became part of the 442nd Regimental Combat team, which was the most decorated in U.S. military history, winning four Distinguished Unit Citations in North Africa, France, and Italy.

On the way to an unknown destination: relocated Japanese-Americans wait at a reception camp.

Scrap rubber was collected for the U.S. war effort. Rubber was one of the few key resources that the United States could not produce itself.

Arsenal of democracy

Japanese planners estimated that the United States could produce ten times as much as Japan. They were wrong; in fact, it produced even more. As the United States geared up for war, its vast natural resources and skilled labor force enabled it to feed and arm twelve million men and women, in addition to helping it support its allies overseas. In 1940 Roosevelt's promise to build 50,000 planes was met with amazement; by 1945, 300,000 had been built.

The U.S. Air Force had 2,470 planes in 1939. By 1944 it had 79,908. In addition, U.S. shipyards turned out 147 carriers and 215 submarines, 952 other warships, 5,200 merchant ships, and 88,000 landing craft. The U.S. Navy expanded twentyfold to become the biggest in the world.

The United States also produced two-thirds of the world's oil supplies. A tenth of all U.S. food production went abroad, mostly to the USSR and to Britain, where the U.S. supplied the millions of U.S. soldiers ready for the invasion of Europe.

Victory at Sea

After inflicting huge damage on the U.S. Pacific fleet at Pearl Harbor, the Japanese captured many Pacific islands. They intended to keep the **Allied Powers** at arm's length, to prevent the bombing of Japan and any interference in their Asian conquests. As the U.S. and its allies fought to roll back Japanese advances, four great naval battles were fought.

Battle of the Coral Sea, May 4–8, 1942

Coral Sea was the first battle in history when opposing fleets never saw each other. Both relied on carrier-based planes as their main weapon. Japan aimed to take Port Moresby, New Guinea, as its base for invading Australia. Because Allied code-breakers read Japan's naval orders, the U.S. Navy knew the Japanese plans. The United States suffered heavier losses, but Port Moresby was saved.

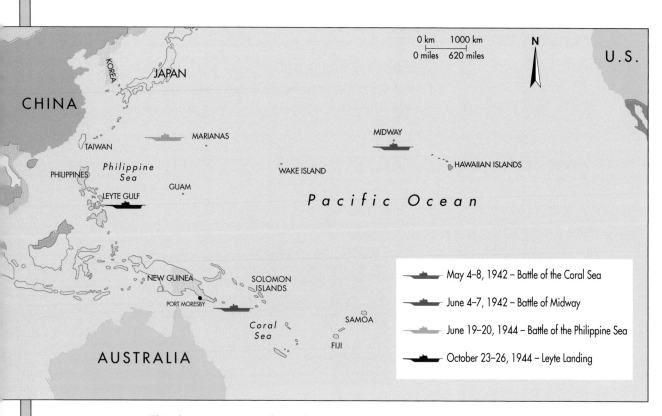

0 km   1000 km
0 miles   620 miles

N

U.S.

KOREA   JAPAN

CHINA

MARIANAS   MIDWAY

TAIWAN   HAWAIIAN ISLANDS

PHILIPPINES   Philippine Sea   WAKE ISLAND

LEYTE GULF   GUAM   Pacific Ocean

NEW GUINEA   SOLOMON ISLANDS

PORT MORESBY   SAMOA

Coral Sea   FIJI

AUSTRALIA

⚓ May 4–8, 1942 – Battle of the Coral Sea
⚓ June 4–7, 1942 – Battle of Midway
⚓ June 19–20, 1944 – Battle of the Philippine Sea
⚓ October 23–26, 1944 – Leyte Landing

This shows major aircraft-carrier battles of the Pacific, 1942–44.

Battle of Midway,
June 4–7, 1942

The Japanese sent 145 ships to take Midway Island, hoping to force the United States to defend it. From Midway they intended to take Hawaii. The United States once again decoded Japanese messages, so U.S. Admiral Chester W. Nimitz could plan accordingly. The Japanese lost four aircraft carriers, a blow from which they never recovered. From Midway onward they could no longer go on the offensive.

A *kamikaze* attack: most *kamikaze* planes were destroyed well before hitting their targets.

Battle of the Philippine Sea,
June 19–20, 1944

The largest carrier battle of the war took place while U.S. troops were fighting for the Mariana Islands, from where Japan could be bombed. Against a much stronger American fleet, the Japanese lost 3 more carriers, 17 submarines, and almost 400 planes—over 90 percent of their remaining carrier-based aircraft.

Battle of Leyte Gulf, October 23–26, 1944

Japan's attempt to prevent U.S. forces from recapturing the Philippines led to the biggest naval battle in history. The Japanese had changed their code, so this time the U.S. fleet did not know of their enemy's intentions. Nevertheless, in a series of actions, U.S. airpower proved decisive. The Japanese lost four carriers and left the U.S. Navy the undisputed master of the Pacific.

Kamikaze

In 1281 and 1284, the Mongol rulers of China sent huge fleets to invade Japan, but they were destroyed by typhoons, which the Japanese called "*kamikaze*" (divine wind). As the war turned disastrously against Japan in 1944, suicide squads were formed to crash their planes on invading ships. Known as *kamikaze* pilots, they sank a U.S. escort carrier at Leyte. When U.S. forces invaded Okinawa, 2,000 *kamikaze* pilots sank 36 ships and damaged 368 more. By the war's end, some 5,000 *kamikaze* had died.

The United States' Japan

The United States advances

U.S. forces bypassed the islands where Japanese forces were strongest. As Japan lost its naval power, these islands could no longer be reinforced or supplied. The first Japanese-held island to be taken, between August 1942 and February 1943, was Guadalcanal in the Solomon Islands. The Japanese managed to evacuate 13,000 troops, abandoning their sick and wounded. Guadalcanal cost around 1,700 U.S. lives and at least 17,000 Japanese lives. In June 1944, U.S. forces took Saipan in the Marianas, from where they could bomb Japan itself. U.S. forces had planned to take Saipan in three days. It took three weeks.

Paying the price

In February 1945, after 72 days of bombing, 110,000 Americans landed on Iwo Jima, an island halfway between Saipan and Japan. They had hoped to take the island in fourteen days—but it took 36. Japanese commanders knew they could not win the war, but hoped the Allies would negotiate for peace, rather than demand Japan's complete surrender. On Okinawa the 172,000 U.S. troops suffered 50,000 casualties. The Japanese lost 110,000 soldiers, plus 150,000 civilians.

Lt. General Richard K. Sutherland (left) accepts Japan's surrender, aboard USS *Missouri*, September 2, 1945.

The end: Destruction

In March 1945, U.S. bombers killed 100,000 civilians in a three-day raid on Tokyo. By May, thirteen million Japanese were homeless. In August the U.S. dropping of atomic bombs on Hiroshima and Nagasaki and the USSR's invasion of Manchukuo finally forced Japan to surrender.

A new beginning: Democracy

For the first time in its history, Japan had been invaded by foreign forces. Under Allied **occupation**, Japan adopted a democratic constitution that guaranteed citizens' rights and gave women the vote. Land was given to peasant farmers. Independent trade unions, mass media, and political parties were allowed. Education was reformed.

Japan's democracy is now more than half a century old. Here, politicians try to catch the voters' interest on the streets during the 1993 elections.

The popular conqueror

General Douglas MacArthur (1880–1964) graduated from West Point military academy with the highest-ever marks. In 1905 he went to Tokyo as assistant to his father, a general. Douglas MacArthur ended World War I as a general himself, with thirteen decorations for bravery. In the 1930s, he organized the Philippine army. In 1942 he lost the Philippines to the Japanese, only to reconquer the islands in 1945. As Supreme Commander of the Allied Powers, MacArthur took charge of the occupation of Japan. A strong supporter of democratic reforms, he became very popular with the Japanese. In 1950 he became Commander-in-Chief of United Nations (UN) forces against **communist** aggression in Korea and organized a daring and successful landing behind enemy lines. When MacArthur called for the bombing of communist China, President Harry S. Truman dismissed him for trying to interfere in a political—rather than military—decision.

Japan's Japan

Wealth...

The occupation of Japan ended in 1952. Some U.S. troops remained because Japan and the United States had become allies. The new constitution drawn up by the Allied Powers for Japan only allowed small forces for self-defense, so it could spend more on building new industries. In 1958 Japan launched the world's largest oil tanker. By 1964 it was wealthy enough to host the Olympics. It started the world's first "bullet-train" service and soon became the world's biggest producer of ships, cars, cameras, radios, and television sets.

The 124-miles- (200-kilometers-) per-hour bullet train is a symbol of Japan's postwar revival.

Later Japan moved away from heavy goods, such as steel and chemicals. These caused pollution and needed large imports of energy and raw materials that Japan did not have. Instead it used its highly educated workers to make computers, photocopiers, and other advanced "light" goods. By 1990 Japan had seven times as many industrial robots as the United States and the world's largest merchant fleet.

...and health

The Japanese became not only richer than ever before but healthier, too. By 2000 life expectancy in Japan was 77 years for men and 83 years for women, compared to 73 and 80 in the United States. The United States has more doctors per person than Japan but spends just over one and a half times as much on health as on defense. Japan spends almost five times as much on health as on defense.

Japan in the world

Japan joined the United Nations in 1956 and remained a close ally of the United States. By the 21st century, it was second only to the United States in giving aid to poor countries and paying for the United Nations.

In the 1970s, Japanese companies began building factories in Southeast Asia, Europe, and North America. By 1992 Japan had invested $386 billion abroad, almost half of it in the United States. The number of Japanese working or studying abroad had grown to 680,000.

Although this development made Japan an economic superpower, it was still not willing or able to use military might overseas. During the 1990–91 Gulf War, for example, it took no part in the fighting, but paid $13 billion toward the cost of liberating Kuwait. It also gave $110 million to help Kurdish refugees and sent pollution experts to help clean up damaged oilfields. In 1992 Japan changed its laws to allow up to 2,000 troops to serve abroad on peaceful UN missions.

The Komatsu factory is in northeast England, the area with the largest concentration of Japanese investment in Europe.

The Great Debate

The rights and wrongs of Japan's surprise attack on Pearl Harbor have been hotly debated. So too is today's position of the United States as the world's police.

Question 1: The attack on Pearl Harbor: was it both criminal and foolish?

Yes!

- Although war is brutal, there are internationally accepted rules to help protect the innocent. An undeclared attack breaks these rules.
- The U.S. government had done its best to avoid war with Japan, trying **diplomacy** and economic sanctions instead.
- The U.S. public did not want war before Pearl Harbor.
- Large-scale modern wars are won by industrial power. Japan should have realised it could not ever hope to defeat the United States in the long run.
- If the Japanese had studied the U.S. way of thinking they would have realised that a sneak attack was the surest way of turning the entire nation against them.

No!

- Feeling that war with the United States was inevitable, was it not just common sense for the Japanese to strike the first blow?
- War is about life and death; it is foolish to think of it as a sport governed by rules of fair play.
- Japan and the United States were of such unequal strength that if the Japanese had waited until the U.S. was ready for war they would have been at an even greater disadvantage.
- The United States was partly to blame for Pearl Harbor by forcing Japan into a corner with economic sanctions.
- Some believe in the "conspiracy theory" that the U.S. government secretly wanted the Japanese attack in order to get public opinion on the side of war.

What do you think?

The United States now has troops and hi-tech aircraft carriers stationed around the world to take action in loca trouble spots. Japan's forces are much more limited.

The world's police

Victory in World War II left the United States and the communist USSR as the world's only superpowers. Between 1947 and 1985 there was dangerous rivalry between them that at times came close to sparking a Third World War. In the end, though, the cost of competing with the United States ruined the Soviet economy and the USSR collapsed. This left the US as the only superpower, a world policeman with troops and bases all round the world.

Question 2: Does it matter if the United States is the only superpower?

Yes!

- If it wishes, the United States can act almost alone—as it did when it invaded Iraq in 2003.
- Although the United States is a democracy, real power rests with its super-rich businesses.
- There is no guarantee that a U.S. president, commander of its armed forces, will act responsibly.
- U.S. economic power is more dangerous but less obvious than its military power.

No!

- The democratic United States sets an example of freedom to all.
- The United States cannot act entirely alone. It has to listen to the European Union, Russia, and China.
- The United States generally behaves responsibly, supporting freedom and good government everywhere.
- Although the United States is very powerful, it is still vulnerable, as the 9/11 terrorist attacks showed.
- The United States usually acts through the United Nations.

What do you think?

Find Out More

Using the Internet

Explore the Internet to find out more about the attack on Pearl Harbor and World War II. You can use a search engine, such as www.yahooligans.com or www.google.com, and type in keywords or phrases such as *Great Depression*, *kamikaze*, *Battle of Midway*, *North Atlantic Treaty Organization*, or *Hiroshima*.

More Books to Read

Becker, Michelle Aki. *World Tour: Japan*. Chicago: Raintree, 2003.

Connolly, Sean. *Witness to History: World War II*.
   Chicago: Heinemann Library, 2003.

Dowswell, Paul. *20th-Century Perspectives: The Causes of World War II*.
   Chicago: Heinemann Library, 2003.

Tames, Richard. *Turning Points in History: Hiroshima: The Shadow of the Bomb*.
   Chicago: Heinemann Library, 2006.

Timeline

1543		First Europeans land in Japan
1639		Japan cuts off foreign trade
1853		U.S. forces Japan to reopen foreign trade
1868		Japan's new government begins modernizing reforms
1890		A. T. Mahan publishes *The Influence of Sea-Power on History*
1894–95		Japan defeats China and takes over Taiwan
1902		Anglo–Japanese alliance
1905		Japan defeats Russia
1904–14		Panama Canal built
1910		Japan takes over Korea
1914–18		World War I
1917		U.S. enters World War I
1919		League of Nations founded at Paris Peace Conference
1922		Washington Naval Conference limits naval building
1924		U.S. bans immigration by Japanese
1929		World trade collapses
1930		London Naval Treaty limits naval building
1931		Japan takes over Manchuria
1932		Manchukuo established
1933		Japan leaves the League of Nations
1937		Japan attempts to conquer all of China
1939		Outbreak of World War II in Europe
1940		Japan takes over French colonies in Southeast Asia
1941	**December 7**	Japan attacks U.S. naval base at Pearl Harbor, Hawaii
1942	**February**	Japan captures Singapore, Britain's main military base in East Asia
	May 4–8	Battle of the Coral Sea
	June 4–7	Japanese navy defeated at Battle of Midway
1943	**February**	U.S. takes Guadalcanal
1944	**June 19–20**	Battle of the Philippine Sea; Saipan taken
	October 23–26	Battle of Leyte Gulf
1945	**March**	U.S. bombers devastate Tokyo
	April	U.S. forces invade Okinawa
	August 6	Atom bomb dropped on Hiroshima
	August 8	USSR declares war on Japan
	August 9	Atom bomb dropped on Nagasaki
	August 14	Japan surrenders
	August 28	U.S. troops land in Japan
1946		Japan adopts a democratic constitution
1949		North Atlantic Treaty Organization founded
1950–53		Korean War
1951		Peace treaty signed between Japan and the United States
1964		Japan hosts Olympic Games
1970		Japan installs first industrial robots
1989		Death of Emperor Hirohito
1998		Japan hosts Winter Olympic Games in Nagano

Glossary

aggression	unprovoked attack
alliance	partnership of friendly nations
Allied Powers	countries fighting together against Germany, Italy, and Japan in World War II; also known as the Allies
ally	nation or state that is friendly to another nation
arsenal	place for storing or making weapons
assassinate	murder, usually for a political reason
attaché	literally "attached," a diplomat with special expert knowledge
casualty	person killed or wounded
colony	land ruled by a foreign government
communist	follower of communism
democracy	system of government based on the equal right of all citizens to choose and change their leaders freely
diplomacy	relations between nations conducted by peaceful means
empire	group of countries ruled by another
evacuate	take to safety
extremist	someone with such strong views that he or she is not prepared to compromise at all
Great Depression	period after the financial panic and collapse of world trade in 1929; the worst was over by 1933
immigration	movement of people into a country
infamy	evil reputation
mobilization	organization of people or resources for war
Nazi	National Socialists Workers' Party in Hitler's Germany
negotiation	settle a problem or dispute by talking and compromise
neutral	on nobody's side
obsolete	completely out of date
occupation	rule by a foreign army
parliament	group responsible for making laws in some countries
plague	disease carried by fleas, often on rats, that is often fatal
puppet government	government that makes no real decisions but is ruled by another authority
reconnaissance	survey of an area to locate the enemy or strategic features
refugee	person forced to move from his or her normal home
sabotage	deliberate damage to stop something from working properly
Soviet	belonging to the Soviet Union (USSR)
surrender	give in, admit defeat
task force	armed force organized for a particular operation
trade union	organization to protect the rights and interests of workers
treachery	betrayal by deception
treaty	official agreement between different countries
unconstitutional	against the laws protecting basic rights
USSR	Union of Soviet Socialist Republics; an empire in which communist Russia controlled neighboring countries from 1917 to 1991; also known as the Soviet Union
yellow fever	acute tropical disease that attacks the liver, heart, and kidneys; it is often fatal

Index